Jacob Sheep

by Julie Murray

Abdo Kids Jumbo is an Imprint of Abdo Kids
abdobooks.com

abdobooks.com

Published by Abdo Kids, a division of ABDO, P.O. Box 398166, Minneapolis, Minnesota 55439.

Printed in the United States of America, North Mankato, Minnesota.

052025

092025

Photo Credits: Adobe Stock, Alamy, Getty Images, Shutterstock

Production Contributors: Teddy Borth, Jennie Forsberg, Grace Hansen
Design Contributors: Candice Keimig, Pakou Moua

Library of Congress Control Number: 2024947612

Publisher's Cataloging-in-Publication Data

Names: Murray, Julie, author.

Title: Jacob sheep / by Julie Murray

Description: Minneapolis, Minnesota : Abdo Kids, 2026 | Series: Fancy farm animals | Includes online resources and index.

Identifiers: ISBN 9798384905240 (lib. bdg.) | ISBN 9798384905943 (ebook) | ISBN 9798384906292 (Read-to-me ebook)

Subjects: LCSH: Jacob sheep--Juvenile literature. | Sheep--Juvenile literature. | Farm animals--Juvenile literature. | Livestock--Juvenile literature. | Domestic animals--Juvenile literature.

Classification: DDC 636.3--dc23

Table of Contents

Jacob Sheep

Jacob sheep are friendly, calm, and smart. They are able to live in very cold weather. These **traits** make them perfect fancy farm animals!

Jacob sheep are not a common **breed**. Their **origins** are unknown. Many people think Jacob sheep came from the Middle East about 3,000 years ago.

Jacob sheep are social animals and need to live in a herd. They are mainly raised on farms for their wool, meat, and skin.

Body

Jacob sheep have a long body with a straight back. They stand about 4 feet (1.2 m) tall. Males weigh up to 180 pounds (82 kg). Females are smaller.

Jacob sheep are known for their special horns. Most Jacob sheep have four horns. Some have two or six! Their horns can stand up or curl around their head.

Jacob sheep have spotted black-and-white **fleece**. They have black cheeks and a black **muzzle**. They have a white patch down the center of their head. This look is often called "badger faced."

Badger

Jacob sheep are **sheared** once a year. They produce about 4 to 6 pounds (1.8 to 2.7 kg) of **fleece** each shearing. The fleece is strong and silky. It is used to make clothes and blankets.

adidas

Diet

Jacob sheep eat grasses, hay, and grains. They help clear **brush** and weeds on farmland. They can eat up to 5 pounds (2.3 kg) of food each day.

Baby Jacob Sheep

Females give birth to one or two babies in the spring. Baby sheep are called lambs. Lambs are about 8 pounds (3.6 kg) at birth. Jacob sheep can live up to 20 years.

More Facts

- Jacob sheep have been **bred** in the British Isles for hundreds of years. Jacob sheep were brought to the United States in the mid-1900s.

- Jacob sheep get their name from the figure Jacob in the Bible. Jacob was a shepherd. His sheep also had black-and-white spotted **fleece**.

- Female Jacob sheep are called ewes. Males are called rams.

Ewe (female)

Glossary

breed – a particular type of animal. To breed an animal is to develop an animal over time for a certain purpose.

brush – a thick group of small trees, shrubs, or bushes growing together.

fleece – the wool coat of an animal.

muzzle – the part of the head of some animals that contains the nose, jaws, and mouth.

origin – the point or place from which something comes.

shear – to trim the fleece or hair from.

trait – a quality that makes an animal different from others.

Index

Visit **abdokids.com** to access crafts, games, videos, and more!